Thunder Moon

poems by

Donna O'Connell-Gilmore

Finishing Line Press
Georgetown, Kentucky

Thunder Moon

Copyright © 2018 by Donna O'Connell-Gilmore
ISBN 978-1-63534-787-6 First Edition
All rights reserved under International and Pan-American Copyright Conventions. No part of this book may be reproduced in any manner whatsoever without written permission from the publisher, except in the case of brief quotations embodied in critical articles and reviews.

ACKNOWLEDGMENTS

"Large Man in a Magazine Photo" appeared in *Willow Springs*
"Grandfather's Bay" and "Goatkeeper's Serpents" appeared in *Cape Cod Poetry Review*
"Song on Your Birthday" appeared in *Glasswork's Menagerie*
"Thunder Moon" and "We Watch Spring from Our Window" appeared in *Off the Coast*
"The Meal" appeared in *The Hopper*
"Giant Steps" appeared in *Tell-tale Inklings # 3*

Publisher: Leah Maines
Editor: Christen Kincaid
Cover Art: Julie Laruvuere
Author Photo: Kara O'Connell
Cover Design: Leah Huete

Printed in the USA on acid-free paper.

Order online: www.finishinglinepress.com
also available on amazon.com

Author inquiries and mail orders:
Finishing Line Press
P. O. Box 1626
Georgetown, Kentucky 40324
U. S. A.

Table of Contents

Second Breath 1
Grandfather's Bay 2
A Marriage 3
Piano in Washington Square Park 4
Grimm Forest 6
Tanzania Summer Camp 8
Giant Steps 9
Bayswater Street 10
Song on Your Birthday 11
A Good Girl's Prize 12
Counterfeit 13
July in the Alps 14
Goat Keeper's Serpents 15
Last One 16
Passage 17
Calm in Bed 18
Thunder Moon 19
The Ribbon Snake and the Sun Porch 20
We Watch Spring from our Window 22
Supplicant 23
You Hover Near Me 24
Uncommon View 25
The Meal 26
Large Man in a Magazine Photo 27
Away 29

To the Strength of My Family

Second Breath

He uncovers the mole behind her ear.
She loves the scary blue one on his inner thigh.
He mentions how her waist puckers
when she snaps shut her tightest jeans.
Her face darkens, green eyes stray.
Her small hand in his drops away.
She vanishes to blow-dry her hair.
She doesn't charge her phone.

Does he dare to place a silver
spiral on her wrist? What if she
presents her back to him, straight
hair shining? He retreats to his
three-decker house, varnishes the stairs.

One gray morning she knocks,
her hair curly in a stream of cold
January rain. Her arms are full.
What if she offers balsam greens
in this first thaw of winter?

Grandfather's Bay

Let me rest by these waters
stirred to turquoise.
Where no waves foment
and no foam smashes the shore.
No wide brimmed voices, no loud umbrellas.

The autumn water is warm.
Pebbles chafe the soles of my feet.
I sink into the brine, tread with deep breath,
splash out as salty as the lung-gilled fish
that first flopped onto land.

My wrinkles are legion.
I sit in the shade of boulders
away from the sun
that coarsens my pores.

Back when you called me Piccola
We drank the sun, and flasks of wine
thinned with water. My thighs and legs
lay over yours, my back braced
against your soft-haired chest.
Leathery fingers combed my long hair.
You ferried me over this sand,
dunked me in this sea, with my legs
circling your waist, my arms around your neck.
I, wet otter, your white beard brushing my face.

We lay wrapped in a worn blanket.
We slept, no sounds but the laugh
of the black faced gulls,
and descending screams of the least terns
bridling to fly south.

A Marriage

Light lilac dress for the opera   a tongue kiss   you called twice next morning

Lobsters bristling on our plates   glass-ceilinged Bateau Mouche down the Seine   I smile up at you   a slight sneer in your eyes greets the camera

Lost in the blizzard   I clutched our baby boy curled in his bunting   older boy locked onto your hand   your voice boomed like a searchlight through my blindness

In our bird rich woods   you imitating the cardinal's macho whistle   I'm an organ playing the veery's sad descending scales

Your fist hammering the table in restaurants   pleading with you to lower your voice   "So What That You Feel Embarrassed!"

Staccato of insults from both sides   my cheeks and neck a rogue blaze   harangue jerking in the air like a hanged man   the children knew they knew   tense sentries on the stairs

Surprise ice storm in Austrian Alps   not daring to peer down from thin height   inching across the glassy ledge   later in the hut we huddled like icicles

Your hands clutching my neck arrange jade discs on a silver cord   reparation for our clenched-jaw drives home after dinner parties

Burgundy on our bedside table   sipping to sleep
I stuffed whimpers in my pillow   I wheedled in my nightgown on my knees

Haze of spring the day I left   waiting by the car as though you would help with the bags

Piano in Washington Square Park

The sun sticks to my smile.
Humans on benches open their coats.
Dobermans and dachshunds
wiggle at each other.

A young woman, her face elaborate
with white and black paint,
checkmates an elder man whose sleeping
bag is busy with holes. He fingers pristine
dreadlocks, grins when our eyes meet.

Rachmaninoff flourishes from an ancient
black Steinway well tuned.
The pianist is tall,
long legs, long arms, long fingers.
He doesn't have to pound,
amplification brims
from the vim in his hands.

He launches into the second
movement of a Chopin Concerto,
my mother's favorite piece.
I see her: Roman-nosed, lips pursed, rapt,
her hands plumped with curved nimble
fingers, her body slightly swaying.

I left too soon for her or me,
we both children
who deserved redress.
My backpack sagged,
I strove to stand erect.

She announced she had dropped
my famed cat Adam —
his penchant for feisty nips,
his ceaseless leaping chair to chair—
somewhere in a city.
With deadly calm
I heard myself say
I would send her
no forwarding address.

Over the years she mentored me
through those black and white keys.
Our shoulders touching,
elbows bumping,
a slight mist on her brow.
After an obdurate winter,
the sun on my face.
The grace of us.

Grimm Forest

I never meant to leave you.
The train huffing and my
mother stern, crackling
like the German conductor
to keep up, get up the stairs .
My breaths like emphysema.
I sat next to my sister,
who wide-eyed the tracks
wizzing by and people waving.

I never meant to leave you.
In the next aisle I glimpsed
My father's skittish
smile he mustered
for my tuckered mother,
but she looked away.
As though they suffered
from a bad flu that hitched
a ride and didn't unhitch.

I clawed my way to a high
berth, stared at the blanched
sky darkening. I drowned
in unquiet sleep, was startled
by a pitch from something
in the black forest
that smacked the window.
Naked trees streaked by.
Giant broomsticks with broken-
off twig fingers that scraped out
debris from eye sockets
when old people were dying.

I didn't fall back to sleep.
The train hurtled through
that forest towards the litter
of a city. I never meant
to leave you. We didn't even
kiss. I stuffed a packet
of my poems into the pocket
of your jeans. You handed me
your jack knife,
a rough D carved on the red handle.
I traced it on that train
throughout that night:
D for Dear, Dear, Dear.

Tanzania Summer Camp

The heat stilled the hours.
We swayed on braided hemp.
Melons, red-fleshed,
hulked on picnic tables
scant with meat. I crammed
my mouth with wedges faster
than the other visitors could eat.
Darkness swooped down,
left me groping for my bed.
The day flared back to me:
earth breaking into black chunks,
two oxen shouldering a harrow
plow, the farmer prodding
with a baobab twig.
I slipped lumps of sweets
between their jowls. Eyes resigned,
nostrils opening and closing,
steam lifting off their flanks.
The night a thick syrup
dripping with sounds:
the lion's curse, the hyena's curdle.
I prayed they'd drop
their dung on mother ground
beneath the tent's long stilts.
Next morning I could poke
with a stick the lion's scattered
droppings, the hyena's heaped.

Giant Steps

Now a host of termites blights the yellow house.
It hunkers on a plain of bleached-out grasses
wearing seed heads light as air.

Back then, on dragged-out afternoons,
I climbed splintery stairs to the attic.
Snarling grown-up voices softened
until I could pretend they were quiet for awhile.
I gazed outside at the rise and hulk of trees
on the horizon, and envisioned other children there,
playing "giant steps" in the shade.

At night the wind stomped
loose clapboards outside my room.
Mornings the meadowlark slurred his whistle,
and the savannah sparrows lisped.
Sometimes I scavenged small flowers
with blue petals and a cinnamon center.
I'd hurry back to the house,
but the flowers fell limp as stunned honeybees.

My skin turned the color of tomatoes.
I hid my face in the dense tall grasses,
never reached the shade of trees.

The house is nailed shut now.
On the horizon high buildings
glaze in the sun.

Bayswater Street

Cheese grater, chunks of romano,
pasta pan massaged to gleaming,
return to pantry shelf.
Nana lathers on the Pond's,
Rolls her huge torso into bed.

She beseeches St. Anthony
to find her cat Bella.
Beads rustling, she repeats
Our Fathers in heaven,
and Mary Immaculates
sitting on his right hand.
She gasps the words.
I, quiet beside her, wondering
if the Father's hand got tired.

Studebaker lights, old Cadillacs
roam across the bedroom curtains,
as boys drive up and down
Bayswater Street, Little Richard
shouting from their radios,
"I got a gal, named Sue,
she knows just what to do!"
Boys broadcasting for girls
who might jerk open the door.
Hard to wait for my turn.

The car is a blue Desoto,
crack in the vent window.
I'm fifteen. The boy lunges at my mouth.
I can hardly catch my breath.
His hand slides up my thigh.
Heat rises. I gasp.
Nana shifts in bed, garlic on her breath.
"Stop! No!" I shove his hand away,
preserving Mary Immaculate,
preventing Satan from poking at my flames.

Song on Your Birthday

Deep pink buds of apple tree
break into pale pink blooms,
conceal the oriole. I hear his notes,
free-ranging, melodious.
He plays a piccolo.

Now he emerges.
His flame-orange feathers
eclipse the apple blossoms,
dazzle against the jet black head,
black wings with startling white bars.

I wonder if he sang this way
the day when you were born,
in this tree younger then, blossoms more profuse,
while I inhaled and pushed the final push,
bloody gush, and couldn't raise my head.

Then your voice, a singing wail, arrested me.
I beheld you wet-skinned, matted hair, blinking.
How you dizzy me.
How you eclipse the bird.

A Good Girl's Prize

Fair-skinned, gray-blue eyes
My hair long thick blonde
The turn of my ankle a gift to a man
My voluminous behind
I crouch here gazing up the hill
Coveting your rich red house
I assumed since I'm a virgin goddess
You'd marry me a good girl's prize
One day I let you nibble
At my million dollar nipples
Through my racy lacey blouse
But your puppy dog jumped up
I slapped it down it yipped
I taught that mongrel a thing or two
What they say about men is true
I promised on our wedding night
If you treated me nice
You could unlock my golden box
And root around in there
But she came along
A squatter on your thighs
Pumped you like a lollypop
With wide-opened eyes
A brunette a bad girl a poet
You've built onto the barn
A poetry salon
She won the house the man
The barn the land
I just don't understand

Counterfeit

You were my host in a tuxedo.
I was your guest of honor in chiffon.
My coiffure highlighted for this occasion.
You did not know I almost did not come.
I joined the throng. I drank Sauvignon Blanc.
I laughed.

Not a belly laugh induced
by a scatological joke,
nor the bonhomie of friends.
It was the masquerade of a diplomat
in a suit and medium heels
at an embassy cocktail party.
Always politic.

You sat at the other head of my table.
Your hair slicked back from the sheen of your brow.
Your nose honed to a point
that could puncture a delicate shell.
Your smile shellacked.

Rather than glare I commended you:
"The roasted red peppers are succulent."
"The mussels in light garlic sauce superb."

When it was time for hugs and good-byes,
I kissed you on the cheek, almost on the mouth.
Judas, short of turning you in.

July in the Alps
1974

Sun in the valley lounged on our faces.
A steep but short up to climb,
light boots, light gloves.
No bouillon packed for delirium.
The trail oozes with mud
merged with a trickle like spittle
from some mountain's ice chin.
Plop of the drip as we climb.

How far? Snow and wind gouge
our features. Straight up like dall
sheep with no hooves and no horns.
Mountains careen upwards.
No beacon for trails to the valley.
Around us white cadavers of rocks.
A scent of sour in my mouth.

We trek horizontal, a narrow iced ledge.
Looking down creates vertigo, hastens our end.
I a beast on all fours that can't feel
its hands or its haunches. Will you leave
the black and blue shins of our marriage behind?
My world is the back of your legs shuffling,
your turnings towards me, your mutterings
lost in the din.

Goat Keeper's Serpents

For months of morning darkness he heard
his goats call "Ah! ah!" for the milking pan,
while he stoked the coal fire, melted the silver,
cooled and hammered, heated and hammered,
old hand holding to the work without smashing a finger.

On her twelfth birthday her father tucked
the dowry bracelet underneath her pillow.
She always wore the silver coil,
on her bare arm around her thin wrist,
like a milk snake's rust bands curling.

She learned how rattlesnakes entwine,
dozens roiling in a den, the female
reverberating to the males' vibrations,
smelling with her tongue until she lifts her tail.

When her time came she'd labor
like a python mother that glides miles
to find an antwarp's hollow,
curls her warmth around her hundred eggs
and gently squeezes till they hatch.

Each night the father spluttered for his breath,
as though the smooth dry rings of a constrictor
gripped his sweaty chest. He prayed she'd be
betrothed before his eyes were pebbles in a skull.

He would leave her the lemon orchard,
though fruit hung lightly on the boughs,
and goats that browsed sparse tufts
of browning grasses waiting for the rain.
He would leave her the silver coil.

Last One

The mustang itches for moisture.
His nostrils search
for a whiff of thunder cloud.
A red clay coat cloaks his body
accented with a shipwreck of ribs.
He stares at rock-strewn terrain.
Acacias, parched as the stallion,
have long lost their leaves
and bared their thorns.
He bends his neck to locoweed,
snorts, not beguiled by its clutch
of purple flowers now blue in death.
Slender ears prick for the thud of hooves.
He harbors the sense
of velvet rumps bumping,
of a herd where a horse
can rest his chin
on another's neck.

Passage

Shorebirds are clearing out.
Pale plovers no longer
camouflage eggs in the sand.
Their chicks no longer wobble,
marshmallows on wispy legs.
I blink and they vanish.

Four automaton sanderlings flee
the antennae of spent whitecaps
creeping up the beach. As the foam
recedes they pursue, siphon
minute moon jellies, sea butterflies
and sea angels marooned in the sand.

The biting greenheads have drowned
in the high tide at August's full moon.
Oystercatchers catch with their carrot beaks.
Gulls with black faces laugh
like echoes from stricken wrecks.
They too will leave before a chill wind stills.

Calm in Bed

Laundered sheets, the night ahead,
my husband's snoring is important.
He's telling me a story in the dark
language and I listen lest I lose the thread.

I hear bumping in the attic
and am not afraid. It's mice scuttling,
their sounds amplified at night. They'll arrange
a nest in the drawer of my great aunt's dresser.
Velvet, warm, amongst the hankies pale and frayed.

Coyotes punctuate our cricket field.
I prick my ears to hear them keen,
chins tilted towards the moon.
They morph to loons wailing in my head,
the couple low-slung in their shining
water bed. The striped collar, the scalloped
back, red eyes, bill for spearing fish.

I glimpse their chicks with downy frizz
huddled under mother's wing
as plush and heated as this quilt
we nestle in. I count one, two,
three...four...I hear her tremolo...

My husband gasps with a start,
then resumes his snores. Perhaps he's
dreaming of our old mower
stuck in the tall grass again.
I barely rest my hand on his chest.

Thunder Moon

Do I dare to rouse you
from the rumpled sheets,
to come and see the peony
under the thunder moon?

She's hiding on a slender stem.
Can we lift her heavy head,
and gaze at untouched folds of lace,
lighted by my blushing face?

The Ribbon Snake and the Sun Porch

A sorority of snowdrops dots the garden,
broccoli buds with crimply leaves emerge.
A breeze quivers the ferny leaves of bleeding hearts.
A young ribbon snake tenders the garden,
scouts for weevils and cut worms,
whiffs the thyme and dill and mint
with its tongue. After a rain
when the garden is damp and cold,
Snake thrusts through an opening
to the sun-porch and toasts its thin
body where sun spills onto the brick floor.

The poet rocks in her chair. Her poetry books—
Stanley Kunitz, Mary Oliver, D. H. Lawrence—
collapse on her lap as she nods into slumber.
A spider skulks in a crack of the brick floor.
Its hairy legs frenzy up her body under her clothes.
Its fangs plunge into her flesh.
Each day she discovers welts in swollen
congregations on her graceful neck,
on her breasts and arms and wrists,
welts that harbor relentless itch.
While she naps she does not notice Snake
meditating as she rocks in her chair:
scratches, composes, and scratches.

Snake spies the spider's errands.
It salivates for this morsel,
but senses it must be agile
as spider is quick. It slips up the poet's
body, eases around her middle,
trembles with readiness.
Spider ascends, Snake springs.
It bites down with small and even teeth,
swallows it whole,
curls up in the corner and meditates.

The poet wakes without an itch.
She beholds the snake: blue stripes
taper down its olive back,
topaz eyes glaze on its head.

She appreciates its elegance and quietude.
Snake surges up her lap and purrs.

She realizes Snake has delivered
her from itch and pestilence.
It has transported grace from the garden
into her writing space. She pets it,
dry and warm as a stone a child
grasps from the beach to skip on water.
It expands and contracts,
while she basks in the sun,
rocks, and writes her manuscript.
In the garden a Carolina wren
cocks its tail with a moth in its beak.
A red fox trots on long black legs.
Japanese primrose rise and hum.

We Watch Spring from our Window

The he-dove scampers on pink legs around and around her,
drags his wings along the ground like a matador his cape,
sings low, almost guttural: "Coo-ah-cooo-cooo-coo".
Her body is plain, brown, still.
She seems to watch and listen,
responds in a whisper "Coo-coo".
His ruff rises like hackles,
the faint blush on his breast blossoms into lilac.

Now she approaches him,
inserts her slender stem of a bill within his.
They bob up and down, up and down,
joined in this cadence.

With a flap of wings he mounts her,
touches cloaca to cloaca,
for one instant, one mass of feathers.
He dismounts. She begins to smooth
his light brown wings, and he hers.
Suddenly, wings whistling, they are gone.
I turn to your touch, light fingers in my hair…

Supplicant

Lord, can you hear this old body implore you?
I cathect the blood in the grooves of your hands.
Come down from the groveling
crowds on the mountainsides.
The veins of tomatoes are pregnant with seeds.
Tables spill over with goats, pullets,
pinks of pig. I breathe in a platter
of poison that purples my breaths.
Will the earth rot or be desert?
Will it be soon? A clock
that limps to its hour.
White wires of madness stir me.
The planets decelerate.
I promise to perpetrate your Word.
Are you coming, Lord?
I am but a shard from your side.

You Hover Near Me

You'd bully on leggings and galoshes.
I'd kick and yank them off.
Instead of making me a lunch
you practiced Fantasy Impromptu.
On the way to school my red ears
heard you banging the black keys.
In the lunchroom someone muttered:
"She has no lunch again."
I gagged on a nickel bottle of watery
milk with a glob of cream at the neck
where a noose would go.

When I defied your curfews,
we flailed at each other's faces.
Two teakettles shrieking with steam.

Some nights it was quiet in the living room.
We took turns reading from your poem
"The Ghosts' and Goblins' Ball."

Near the end I went to you. I wore a purple scarf.
For a decade your mind spooked by tumbleweed,
this hour you found some rest.
Your eyes teared, met mine and never wavered.
Your lips moved as if in earnest conversation,
softened into hints of smiles.
I told you "How beautiful you are!"
large brown eyes, coarse white curls,
even the Roman nose you bemoaned.
How your poems were my sinew, muscle to bone:

....The wind furnished music in minor off key,
through a crack in the old barn door,
....and the ghosts started waltzing
and slow somersaulting
without ever touching the floor....

Uncommon View

Over tequilas
a stranger confided about another,
dearer path to see The Canyon.
A locked gate, a dirt road, a hike in.

The woods filled with elk.
A bull so close
we pretended not to see,
but drank him with a quick thirst:
tall as rafters in a church,
his rack rattling the branches,
his thick neck reaching for leaves
beginning to color.
We walked a sudden rise to the clearing.

My heart clattered,
can't you hear it?
The lugs on my boots gripped the ground.
You stood at the brink,
legs apart framing the gaping hole.
With extended hand
you invited me to join.
No. No.

I tried to look around.
Rock walls surged.
The sun cast its shadow,
vivid rust and gold,
timid pinks and greens.
I stared, locked on to those canyons.
I imagined ancients,
squat, not airy, closer to the ground,
standing easy on the brinks.

My eyes, emboldened,
scanned eons down.
I found the river, a scratchy line.

The Meal

A family of crows assembles in the deep snow.
The wind ripped through their roost last night,
the choice crabapples of summer freeze at their feet.

In its den the snake's skin shrivels
while new skin shines the color of embers.
Come spring the snake will surge from old skin
and flash across the rocks, a begging target.
The black bulk of crow will dive into the blow,
the black beak will flip it and hack it.
There's this sweet morsel in the middle of the belly.
Piquant, pink, and plump.

The crows press close together against the wind.
Their eyes roll back into their skulls and
gaze at the blaze on the rocks.

Large Man in a Magazine Photo

I'm drawn to you in black and white.
The way you don't lean, your cane a companion.
Your thick camel hair coat wraps
around your girth. Your lips a tight
line certain of the right way to go.

Unlike you, father was an ordinary
man and thin as a maple sapling.
If he met you he would call you "sir",
speak up only if invited.
Gray hair careless on his forehead.
He wore a jacket until a zipper broke
or loose buffalo nickels
escaped through his pockets.
When I'd ask about his day
at the Raytheon factory
he'd be silent and ruffle my hair.
At mother's bidding he scrubbed
the rings around the bathtub on his knees.
If her voice leapt an octave
he was the one who said "I'm sorry."

If I were your child I could have gazed
up at you rather than see my father gaze down.
I could bend my neck way back to view
paintings of rams with curling horns
on the domed ceiling of your offices.

Did you have children?
My father ferried us
on his back throughout the house
when we played "whoa and giddy-up".
He regaled us at bedtime,
tales about childhood told with a hint of lilt,

with wide-mouthed grins and dimples.
On his last bed young grandkids
climbed the thin trunk of his body.
Their murmurings like quiet bells.

Away

The cat waits at the window
for your thin figure striding up the walk,
hole in jeans at the knee, crisp blue shirt I too like to wear,
baseball cap harboring gray hair the barber butchered.

The great horned owl calls at dusk,
a ventriloquist—out in our pines or miles away?
I strew dishes in the sink, squint
at the World Series from your recliner.

I go to bed. It's quiet. You're not playing
zombie on the other pillow, slack-jawed,
with a glassy-eyed death stare.
I'll save you The Times article on Afghanistan.

I slip out to the dark porch, hear the owl again.
He's courting at this time of year. Any night now
she'll flirt back, six hoots to his five.
She'll brood eggs by December.

The cat trounced his catnip-flavored mouse,
boozed around in it, dozed belly-up.

Your voice husky, elated in last night's call:
ravens hoarse and rowdy in the canyon,
swooping and somersaulting in the abyss.

On our first date, you played a wolf howls cassette
in your old Isuzu. We drove, transfixed, for half an hour.
Your hand reached for mine, your other steady at the wheel.
Your hands were smooth for a man's, your nails
impeccable, like the interior of that old Isuzu.
You say you'll be delayed the next three days.

In bed, the cat's frame leans against mine.
I strain to hear the owls. The moon is tin.

Personal Acknowledgments

My appreciation goes to my special mentors: Tom Daley of Cambridge and Keith Althaus of Castle Hill in Truro for their interest, patience, and splendid training; and to outstanding teachers at the Fine Arts Work Center in Provincetown: Sarah Eliza Johnson, Fred Marchant, Cleopatra Mathis, Daisy Freid and Martha Collins.

Also thanks to my friends and colleagues in poetry groups: Marjorie Block, Susan Web, Beeby Pearson, Lucile Burt, Ginia Pati, Leo Thibault, Chuck Medansky, Wilderness Sarchild and Diane Ashley, for their thoroughness and understanding.

Finally, thanks to my husband Jon and my sons Karl and Greg for their faithful encouragement and support.

Donna O'Connell-Gilmore earned her MA in clinical social work and developed a psychotherapy practice in the rural suburbs west of Boston, MA. She also wrote a long-running weekly column in regional newspapers about birds and birding.

In the late 1990's she moved to the shores of Cape Cod and began to seriously write poetry. Donna's poems have been published in *Willow Springs, Blueline Journal, The Hopper, Off the Coast, Cape Cod Poetry Review, Written River, Glassworks, Provincetown Magazine, Prime Time, Tell-Tale Inklings# 3, Big Windows Review, Turtle Island Quarterly,* and other literary journals. *Broadsided Press* exhibited her work on Cape Cod buses.

Her chapbook *Africa is the Mother Who Lies in the Grass: poems on safari* won second place from *Writer's Digest* for best self-published poetry collection. In two successive years, she won first place in the Katherine Lee Bates Poetry Fest, and she won first place in The Women's Association's "In Her Own Voice." She was a regional winner in the Joe Gueveia Outermost Poetry Contest.

On the radio she has analyzed her poems about intimacy in couple and family relationships. She is a regular at open mics on the cape and she maintains a part-time practice of psychotherapy. She is passionate about critters and her email reads "wolvesaregods."

www.ingramcontent.com/pod-product-compliance
Lightning Source LLC
LaVergne TN
LVHW040117080426
835507LV00041B/1453